Conjunctions

so...

or?

but...

written by Ann Heinrichs

illustrated by Dan McGeehan and David Moore

The Child's World®

Published by The Child's World®
1980 Lookout Drive • Mankato, MN 56003-1705
800-599-READ • www.childsworld.com

ACKNOWLEDGMENTS
The Child's World®: Mary Berendes, Publishing Director
The Design Lab: Design and page production
Red Line Editorial: Editorial direction

LIBRARY OF CONGRESS CATALOGING-IN-PUBLICATION DATA
Heinrichs, Ann.
  Conjunctions / by Ann Heinrichs ; illustrated by Dan McGeehan and
David Moore.
    p. cm.
  Includes bibliographical references and index.
  ISBN 978-1-60253-427-8 (library bound : alk. paper)
  1. English language—Conjunctions—Juvenile literature. I. McGeehan,
Dan, ill. II. Moore, David, ill. III. Title.
  PE1345.H453 2010
  428.2—dc22   2010011457

Printed in the United States of America in Mankato, Minnesota.
March 2013
PA02180

ABOUT THE AUTHOR

Ann Heinrichs was lucky. Every year from grade three through grade eight, she had a big, fat grammar textbook and a grammar workbook. She feels that this prepared her for life. She is now the author of more than 100 books for children and young adults. She has also enjoyed successful careers as a children's book editor and an advertising copywriter. Ann grew up in Fort Smith, Arkansas, and lives in Chicago, Illinois.

ABOUT THE ILLUSTRATORS

Dan McGeehan spent his younger years as an actor, author, playwright, cartoonist, editor, and even as a casket maker. Now he spends his days drawing little monsters!

David Moore is an illustration instructor at a university who loves painting and flying airplanes. Watching his youngest daughter draw inspires David to illustrate children's books.

TABLE OF CONTENTS

What Is a Conjunction?

That gorilla is huge but friendly.

We won the game and got the trophy.

I want cookies, so I will go bake some.

Is Sparky in his doghouse or on my bed?

The colored words are **conjunctions**. Conjunctions link words together. They show how two or more ideas in a sentence **connect** to each other.

Imagine these sentences without their conjunctions.
The sentences don't make sense!

That gorilla is huge friendly.

We won the game got the trophy.

I want cookies I will go bake some.

Is Sparky in his doghouse on my bed?

There are seven basic conjunctions: and, or, but,
nor, yet, so, for.

And, Or, But

You use and, or, and but all the time.
Use and to add things together.

I'd like sprinkles and cherries
on my sundae, please!

But shows how things are different.

I can play soccer, but I can't swim.

Use or when there's a choice between things.

Would you like to watch a
movie or play a game?

Nor, Yet, So, For

We use nor instead of *or* when neither choice will do.

Neither the pink dress nor the blue one fit her.

Yet is **similar** to *but*.

I'm tired, yet I cannot sleep.

So shows how one thing causes another.

I want to play, so I'm going outside.

For tells why something happened.

I got the lead role, for I am a good actor.

I want dinner, so I'm going to cook some.

Putting Things Together

Conjunctions can join words together.

The *mother* and *baby* went for a walk.

Conjunctions can join groups of words.

My goldfish jumped *out of its tank* and *into my shoe.*

Conjunctions can make two sentences into one.

Close the door. Please don't slam it.
Close the door, and please don't slam it.

And . . . And . . . And . . .

Conjunctions give us a shorter, easier way to say things. We don't have to repeat extra words.

The monster likes broccoli. The monster likes spinach. The monster likes broccoli and spinach.

The teacher is strict. The teacher is kind. The teacher is strict but kind.

You don't have to repeat the conjunction, either. You probably wouldn't say, "I'll have mustard and ketchup and pickles and relish and peppers and onions, please!" You'd say:

I'll have mustard, ketchup, pickles, relish, peppers, and onions, please!

I am running, jumping, skipping, and hopping to try to catch you.

You can replace all of those extra conjunctions with **commas** (,). Sometimes, though, it's useful to repeat the word and to make a point:

That dog of yours just barks and barks and barks!

I keep running and running and running.

More Connections

Many other words can connect ideas in other ways. Some kinds of conjunctions have two or more words. Some put events in order.

I like a snack before I go to bed.

I'll clean my room after I'm finished with practice.

First	Second
have a snack	go to bed
practice	clean my room

Conjunctions can also show how things happen
at the same time.

I made you a present while you were sleeping.

I laugh whenever I see monkeys.

I like to
shower after
I exercise.

Some kinds of conjunctions can show how one thing leads to another.

I'll go on the roller coaster if you come with me.

Others help you explain things:

I like kangaroos because they're so bouncy.

I'm going outside even though it is raining.

Conjunctions help combine and **compare** things, too:

We could order both hamburgers and pizza for dinner.

The Right Conjunction

Changing the conjunction can change the meaning of the sentence. What happens to these sentences when you change the conjunction?

I eat grapes and bananas for lunch. (or)

I eat a snack before I go to bed. (after)

I eat my snack after I go to bed!

How to Learn More

AT THE LIBRARY

Cleary, Brian P. *But and For, Yet and Nor: What Is a Conjunction?*
Minneapolis, MN: Millbrook, 2010.

Fisher, Doris, and D. L. Gibbs. *Tennis Court Conjunctions*. Pleasantville, NY:
Gareth Stevens, 2008.

Heller, Ruth. *Fantastic! Wow! and Unreal!: A Book About Interjections and
Conjunctions*. New York: Puffin Books, 2000.

McClarnon, Marciann. *Painless Junior Grammar*. Hauppauge, NY: Barron's
Educational Series, 2007.

Schoolhouse Rock: Grammar Classroom Edition. Dir. Tom Warburton.
Interactive DVD. Walt Disney, 2007.

ON THE WEB

Visit our home page for lots of links about grammar: *childsworld.com/links*

NOTE TO PARENTS, TEACHERS AND LIBRARIANS: We routinely check our Web links to make sure they're
safe, active sites—so encourage your readers to check them out!

Glossary

commas (KOM-uhs): Punctuation marks that break up parts of sentences. You use a comma with some conjunctions.

compare (kum-PAIR): To notice what is the same and what is different between two or more things. Some conjunctions help compare two or more things.

conjunctions (kuhn-JUNGK-shuns): Words that join words or sentences together. The seven basic conjunctions are *and*, *but*, *or*, *nor*, *yet*, *so*, and *for*.

connect (kuh-NEKT): To join together two or more things. Conjunctions connect parts of sentences.

similar (SIM-uh-lur): Things are similar when they are alike or almost the same. Some conjunctions show how things are similar.

Index